Anglo-Saxons & VIKINGS

INVADERS & CONQUERORS

BY
AMY ALLATSON

©2016
Book Life
King's Lynn
Norfolk PE30 4LS

ISBN: 978-1-78637-003-7

All rights reserved
Printed in Spain

A catalogue record for this book
is available from the British Library.

Written by:
Amy Allatson MA
(History & Culture)

Edited by:
Grace Jones

Designed by:
Drue Rintoul

CONTENTS

Words in red can be found in the glossary on page 31.

Britain's first INVADERS

The Romans were the first invaders of Britain; they stayed for over 350 years. They invaded in the year A.D. 43 and successfully conquered much of Britain from the native Celts. Many Celtic tribes fought back against the Romans. Some, however, bargained with the Roman leaders by promising peace in return for their kingdoms.

Roman Britain

The Romans brought many influences with them, much of which are still visible in Britain today. Many roads in Britain were made by the Romans and are recognisable for their long length and straightness. The Romans also left behind many buildings and structures, some of which are still standing today.

THE SOLAR CALENDAR

THE ROMANS INVENTED THE CALENDAR WE USE TODAY. IT IS BASED ON THE MOVEMENT OF THE EARTH AROUND THE SUN. THE TWELVE MONTH NAMES ARE TAKEN FROM ROMAN GODS, GODDESSES AND RULERS. ROMAN EMPEROR, JULIUS CAESAR, NAMED THE MONTH OF JULY AFTER HIMSELF.

IN CHESTER, THE ROMAN WALLS CAN STILL BE SEEN THROUGHOUT THE CITY. SOLDIERS WOULD PATROL AROUND THE OUTSIDE OF THE WALLS TO KEEP THE CITY SAFE. THE ROMANS HAD DIFFERENT NAMES FOR OUR CITIES AND TOWNS, LONDON WAS CALLED LONDINIUM.

DID YOU KNOW...?

THE ROMANS INVADED BRITAIN TWICE BEFORE THEIR SUCCESSFUL INVASION IN A.D. 43, ONCE IN 55 B.C. AND IN 54 B.C.

B.C. IS AN ABBREVIATION OF "BEFORE CHRIST". A.D. IS LATIN FOR "ANNO DOMINI", WHICH MEANS, AFTER CHRIST'S BIRTH.

ROMAN BATHS IN BATH

A MAP OF THE ROMAN EMPIRE. →

The Roman Empire

The Roman Empire was extensive. The Romans controlled many European countries such as modern day France, Spain and Italy, as well as parts of Africa and Asia. Despite their large empire, by the end of the 4th Century, Rome's authority had been consistently challenged and the Empire's power was in decline.

Roman Withdrawal

Barbarian invaders had begun to attack not only Britain's shores, but other parts of the empire as well. The Roman army was called away from Britain by the Emperor Honorius and sent to other parts of the empire to tackle the barbarian threat. The Roman army left Britain in A.D. 410, leaving the native Britons vulnerable to invasion once again.

HOW DO WE KNOW...?

THE ROMANS BEGAN DOCUMENTING THE EVENTS THAT HAPPENED AND THE PEOPLE WHO LIVED IN THEIR EMPIRE. THEY CREATED A CENSUS TO COUNT THE POPULATION OF EACH AREA, A SYSTEM STILL USED TODAY.

A RE-ENACTMENT OF ROMAN SOLDIERS MARCHING.

Who were the ANGLO-SAXONS & VIKINGS?

The Anglo-Saxons were tribes made up of three main groups; the Jutes, Angles and Saxons. The Angles and the Saxons were the two largest tribes that came to Britain; this is why we know them today as the Anglo-Saxons.

Changing Beliefs

The Romans brought Christianity to Britain during their settlement; the Anglo-Saxons, however, were Pagans. They brought with them their own set of beliefs and Gods. Roman culture had left its mark on Britain; both the Romans and the Anglo-Saxons had brought two unique cultures and beliefs to Britain. Over time, the two moulded into a new culture with a new set of beliefs.

Anglo-Saxon Roles

Anglo-Saxon women were central to the running of the home and farms. Anglo-Saxon women were also very skilled in textile work, often making clothes for the family and to sell. Men and boys who were old enough usually worked on the farms, although women frequently helped. Both were skilled craftsmen working mostly with wood and iron to make tools and jewellery.

DID YOU KNOW...?

THE WORD 'VIKING' COMES FROM A LANGUAGE CALLED OLD NORSE AND MEANS 'A PIRATE RAID'.

FREYJA, THE ANGLO-SAXON GODDESS OF LOVE AND WAR WAS KNOWN AS 'FRIGG' TO THE VIKINGS. SHE IS OFTEN PORTRAYED RIDING A CHARIOT PULLED BY TWO GIANT CATS!

The VIKINGS

The Vikings came from parts of Scandinavia, including Norway, Denmark and Sweden. They travelled by ships, called longboats, to places around modern day Europe in search of land and treasure.

Raids on Britain

The Vikings led raids on Britain, fought the Anglo-Saxons, stole from villages and looted monasteries. They eventually started to conquer and control Britain almost one hundred years after the first raids began. Some Vikings came for this purpose, whilst others came peacefully to settle and farm the land.

EXPLORERS

The Vikings were keen adventurers and explorers. They sailed the seas in longships to buy goods such as spices, silver and wine to bring back home.
The Vikings explored much of the world and travelled huge distances. They travelled through Russia to get to the Middle East and also as far as North America!

VIKINGS DECORATED THEIR LONGSHIPS WITH CARVINGS OF MYTHICAL CREATURES, LIKE DRAGONS, TO SCARE ENEMIES.

A VIKING LONGSHIP.

DID YOU KNOW...?

THE VIKINGS WERE ALSO PAGANS. THEIR GODS WERE SIMILAR TO THE ANGLO-SAXON GODS. THE MAIN VIKING GOD, ODIN, WAS CALLED WODEN BY THE ANGLO-SAXONS.

The Anglo-Saxon INVASION

From the year A.D. 449, Britain came under attack from the large numbers of Anglo-Saxon warriors invading by boat.

Raids on Britain

They began to attack the coastline of Britain, armed with swords, spears and round shields. Some Britons fought back with terrible results; many lives were lost. Most, however, were pushed out of their lands and into the North of England.

GILDAS

We know about the Anglo-Saxon invasion because an English priest called Gildas, recorded the events as they happened. He wrote 'that the invaders did not stop their attack until they had captured most of southern Britain'.

A REPLICA OF ANGLO-SAXON ARMOR.

AN ILLUSTRATION OF AN ANGLO-SAXON INVASION.

Map of the Anglo-Saxon INVASION

Northumbria

Mercia

Anglia

Wessex

Kent

DARK Ages

The period of time after the Romans withdrew from Britain is sometimes known as the 'Dark Ages'. This is because it is seen as a period in which there were few technological discoveries and little progress. The term is also used to explain how little we know of the period because there had been little written down on paper during this time.

STAINED GLASS FROM THE DARK AGES.

The Anglo-Saxon KINGDOMS

After the Anglo-Saxons successfully conquered England, they slowly divided it into separate kingdoms, each with a different ruler. They pushed the native Celts into parts of Wales, Scotland and Cornwall.

Northumbria

Mercia

Anglia

Wessex

Kent

The five main kingdoms were: Northumbria, Mercia, Wessex, Kent and Anglia. Each had their own warrior king and army. You can recognise some of the names from modern day place names in England, such as Anglia, which is now called East Anglia.

	Northumbria
	Mercia
	Anglia
	Wessex
	Kent

10

Anglo-Saxon CONTROL

Although the Britons fought back against the invaders, by A.D.600, much of the South and East of Britain was controlled by the Anglo-Saxons. They brought with them their own style of housing, clothing and language.

A REPLICA OF AN ANGLO-SAXON SHIELD.

A RE-ENACTMENT OF AN ANGLO-SAXON ARMY.

A RECOVERED ANGLO-SAXON SWORD.

DID YOU KNOW...?

THE COUNTRIES OF ENGLAND, SCOTLAND AND WALES DID NOT EXIST DURING ANGLO-SAXON TIMES. SCOTLAND AND WALES WERE TRIBE LANDS CONTROLLED BY THE PICTS AND CELTS. IT WASN'T UNTIL MUCH LATER THAT ENGLAND WAS UNIFIED BY THE ANGLO-SAXON KING, ETHELSTAN WHO WAS THE FIRST KING OF ALL ENGLAND IN A.D. 927.

The Viking RAIDS

The Vikings were trained warriors and attacked Britain's monasteries, as they held great wealth and no religious significance to the Vikings. Many Vikings continued raiding parts of Britain and other countries, but some began to settle in Britain.

Longships Arrive

Around A.D. 789 the first recorded Viking attack took place. Three Viking longships arrived on the South coast of England. A local Reeve was sent out to greet the newcomers, and was killed instantly; a long period of Viking terror had begun.

DID YOU KNOW...?

VIKINGS WERE KNOWN AS 'NORSE' OR 'NORSEMEN'. THIS IS BECAUSE THEY CAME FROM THE NORTH OF MODERN DAY EUROPE, AND SPOKE THE LANGUAGE OLD NORSE.

DID YOU KNOW...?

VIKING HELMETS DID NOT HAVE HORNS.

European ATTACK

The Vikings not only attacked Britain, but the coastlines of Europe and parts of Asia too, including large and wealthy cities, such as Paris and Constantinople.

Anglo-Saxon CHRONICLE

The first Viking raid was recorded in the Anglo-Saxon Chronicle. The Chronicle became a very useful book from the Anglo-Saxon period because little had been written during the 'dark ages'. The Chronicle documents a fierce struggle between Anglo-Saxons and Vikings as they fought for power and control of Britain.

PART OF THE ANGLO-SAXON CHRONICLE

VIKING SIEGE ON PARIS

LINDISFARNE

In A.D. 793, the Vikings attacked a Christian monastery at Lindisfarne located on the North-East coast of England. Lindisfarne was a holy island where many **monks** lived and worked at the monastery. Before the Vikings attacked, Northumbria was under Anglo-Saxon rule.

The Monastery

At the start of the year A.D. 793, Viking longships were seen approaching the shore and soon after the Vikings attacked. The monastery housed many precious books, art and treasures. The Vikings burnt down buildings, killed the monks and stole valuable items, such as gold.

PART OF THE HIGHLY DECORATED LINDISFARNE GOSPEL

Surprise ATTACK

The attack on Lindisfarne was a surprise, achieved with only a small number of longships. The Vikings knew there would be little resistance to their attack, as the monks who lived on the island were unprepared and unarmed. After the attacks, the Vikings travelled home on their ships with their stolen goods.

The Vikings
ARE HERE TO STAY...

Summer raids became a frequent occurrence; the Vikings would return home for winter with their treasure. Summer was a popular time for raiding for the seafaring Vikings, due to fewer storms, warmer weather and changes in wind direction. By the A.D. 850s, the Viking raiders did not leave after a summer of raiding. Instead, they set up camp near the shore for winter so they would be ready to attack again the following summer.

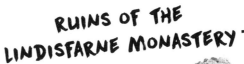

RUINS OF THE LINDISFARNE MONASTERY

15

Fighting between the ANGLO-SAXONS & THE VIKINGS

Viking raids on Britain continued for many years, as did the fighting between the Anglo-Saxons and the Vikings. The Vikings had many victories and within a few years they began to settle on the land they had conquered. However, the Vikings wanted to rule all of England and the fight for land still continued.

Vikings INVADE!

In A.D. 865 a large army of Vikings known as the 'Great Heathen Army' invaded Britain. They were a group of warriors from Sweden, Norway and Denmark who came together to invade the Anglo-Saxon kingdoms of Northumbria, Mercia, Anglia and Wessex.

Once again England was divided. The Vikings controlled much of the North and East whilst the Anglo-Saxons held much of the South.

REPLICA VIKING HELMET AND ARMOR

VIKING INVASIONS
from the 8th to 9th century

The Capture of BRITAIN

The Viking army stayed in England for over ten years, fighting the English kings and taking control of their kingdoms. There was a long and bloody power struggle between the Anglo-Saxons and the Vikings for control over various kingdoms. But, by the end of the invasion, the Vikings had captured large parts of England and began to settle on the land that they had conquered.

DID YOU KNOW...?

THE 'GREAT HEATHEN ARMY' WAS LED BY RAGNAR LODBROK, KING OF THE SWEDES, AND HIS SONS; IVAR THE BONELESS AND SIGURD SNAKE-IN-THE-EYE. AS THEIR NAMES CLAIM, THEY WERE ALL FEARSOME WARRIORS!

Jorvik

In A.D. 867 the Vikings captured a piece of land the Anglo-Saxons called Eoforwic. The Vikings renamed the land Jorvik. This city is known today as York. Jorvik became the capital of Danelaw. The invasion did not stop here, during A.D. 892 over two-hundred and fifty Viking longships invaded to fight King Alfred of Wessex.

HOW DO WE KNOW...?

NO ONE KNOWS FOR SURE HOW BIG THE VIKING ARMY WAS. HOWEVER, HISTORIANS ESTIMATE THERE WERE AROUND TWENTY MEN IN EACH SHIP WHICH WOULD MEAN OVER FIVE THOUSAND VIKING WARRIORS TOOK PART IN THE SECOND INVASION OF ENGLAND.

AN ILLUSTRATION OF THE INVASION OF THE VIKINGS.

King Alfred
THE GREAT

The Anglo-Saxon king, Alfred, was born in A.D. 849. Alfred succeeded his brother Ethelred, who died in battle, to become King of Wessex. Alfred inherited not just the power and wealth of Wessex – the last Anglo-Saxon Kingdom – but also, the struggle to keep control from the Vikings. He is known today for defending England against the Viking invasion, enforcing new laws and translating Latin documents into English so they could be preserved.

DID YOU KNOW...?

ALFRED CLAIMED TO BE KING OF ALL ENGLAND AND IS THE ONLY ENGLISH KING TO BE DEEMED GREAT.

TRUTH OR MYTH?

LEGEND HAS IT THAT KING ALFRED, WHEN IN HIDING FROM THE DANES, ONCE BURNT SOME CAKES (SMALL LOAVES OF BREAD) BY FAILING TO TAKE THEM OUT OF THE OVEN. THE PEASANT WOMAN WAS SAID TO HAVE SCOLDED ALFRED, NOT REALISING HE WAS THE KING.

Alfred Vs THE VIKINGS

Alfred became King of Wessex in A.D. 871. His brothers and family before him had a long history of fighting the Vikings. Alfred continued this fight and after many losses, won a battle at Edington (modern day Wiltshire) in A.D. 878. This battle resulted in a group of Vikings agreeing to live in peace under Danelaw, although, for the larger part, fighting continued elsewhere.

DID YOU KNOW...?

ALFRED COLLECTED AND PUT TOGETHER THE LAWS OF KINGS BEFORE HIM. THIS BECAME BRITAIN'S FIRST SET OF OFFICIAL LAWS.

A PORTRAIT OF KING ALFRED.

Danish ENGLAND

The areas the Vikings settled in were known as Danelaw. They were allowed to rule these areas by the Anglo-Saxon kings. The Vikings were also allowed to follow their own laws and traditions in these areas.

Danelaw

DID YOU KNOW...?

DANELAW WAS DEFINED IN A TREATY IN A.D. 880 BETWEEN THE VIKING KING, GUTHRUM, AND THE ANGLO-SAXON KING, ALFRED.

Viking LANDS

The Vikings controlled many areas that would now be considered the Midlands; Leicester, Lincoln, Nottingham, Derby and Stamford. Now the Vikings held control over these areas, they began to farm the land, as the Anglo-Saxons had done years earlier.

THE MODERN DAY CITY OF YORK, KNOWN TO THE VIKINGS AS 'JORVIK'.

Meanwhile...

In A.D. 899, Alfred died and his son Edward, known as Edward the Elder, took over as King of Wessex. What remained of Mercia was ruled by his sister Ethelflaed. Ethelflaed is referred to as 'Lady of the Mercians' for her part in defending the kingdom against the Vikings. She built many fortresses to protect Mercia and was known for being a strong leader.

A PAINTING OF KING EDWARD THE ELDER, SON OF ALFRED.

A PAINTING OF ETHELFLAED.

DID YOU KNOW...?

THE VIKINGS GAVE NEW NAMES TO THE PLACES THEY CONQUERED, SOME OF WHICH ARE STILL USED TODAY. THIS INCLUDES NAMES ENDING WITH 'TOFT', SUCH AS LOWESTOFT OR 'KIRK', SUCH AS ORMSKIRK.

Reclaiming LAND

Alfred's children, Edward and Ethelflaed, were able to reclaim some of Danelaw from the Vikings. They reclaimed some of the captured land, although the Vikings who remained in these areas still kept their own customs.

Changing RULERS

The years that followed were ones of **turbulent** change in leadership. By A.D. 926, much of the East of England was recaptured by the Anglo-Saxons.

King CANUTE

By A.D. 1016, Danish King Canute had led yet another Viking invasion, again attacking and successfully capturing Wessex which was at this point ruled by the Anglo-Saxon king, Edmund.

Edmund IRONSIDE

Edmund, known as Edmund Ironside was the son of King Ethelred. In the face of Viking attack, Edmund's father, Ethelred, had tried to stop the Vikings from invading by giving them land and money. This became known as Danegeld. The Vikings accepted Ethelred's offer but still continued with their attack. Fighting continued between Edmund's army and Vikings all over the country. After much fighting, King Canute took control over England after the Battle of Assandun in A.D. 1016.

Edward the Confessor and the NORMAN CONQUEST

In A.D. 1042, Anglo-Saxon England saw a new king, Edward the Confessor, take to the throne. He was the son of Ethelred and had been exiled to Normandy years before. This was due to the Danish invasion which made it unsafe for him to remain in the country. On return to England, he regained his family's claim to the throne. Edward went on to marry an Anglo-Saxon noblewoman, Edith of Wessex, and strengthened his rule. Despite this, Edward died without an **heir**, leaving England without a clear leader once again.

A DRAWING FROM THE ANGLO- SAXON CHRONICLE, DEPICTING EDMUND IRONSIDE (LEFT) AND CANUTE (RIGHT) FIGHTING.

Claim to the THRONE

When Edward died in A.D. 1066 there were three claims to the throne.

Who do you think had the strongest claim to the throne?

Harold Godwinson, Earl of Wessex	William, Duke of Normandy	Harald Hardrada, King of Norway
A powerful nobleman, according to the Anglo-Saxon Chronicle, Edward named him as his "true" successor on his death bed.	It was reported that Edward had promised his distant relative the throne. He was a blood relative, but the throne was not hereditary at this point in history.	Based his claim on the fact that his ancestor, King Canute, had once ruled England (1016-1035).

The Norman CONQUEST

Noblemen, known as witan, declared Harold Godwinson King of England. William of Normandy and Harald Hardrada, the King of Norway, were not happy with the decision. They both believed they had the true claim to the throne.

THE BAYEUX TAPESTRY DEPICTING THE NORMAN CONQUEST.

1066 Battle of HASTINGS

In A.D. 1066, England was invaded by a Norwegian army, led by Harald Hardrada, who landed in the north. Harold Godwinson's men killed Harald Hardrada in a battle at Stamford Bridge. Days later William's Norman army landed in Sussex. Harold hurried south and the two armies fought in the Battle of Hastings. The Normans won, Harold was killed, and William became king. This brought an end to Anglo-Saxon and Viking rule. Britain now had a Norman king.

DID YOU KNOW...?

KING WILLIAM WAS KNOWN AS 'WILLIAM THE CONQUEROR' DUE TO HIS CONQUEST OF ENGLAND.

How did the Anglo-Saxons AND VIKINGS LIVE?

Anglo-Saxon HIERARCHY

The king was the most powerful person in Anglo-Saxon times. Next came the thanes (nobles) who helped the king to rule. Poorer people were called churls. These free people fought for the thanes and worked on the land. Slaves were beneath them.

Religion

The Anglo-Saxons were pagans with their own gods, such as the chief god, Woden and Frigg the goddess of love. During the course of settlement, the Anglo-Saxons did convert to Christianity and we have Anglo-Saxon churches still standing today.

Where did THEY LIVE?

Kings lived in big wooden houses, called halls. They were built to be impressive structures to showcase their power and influence over their kingdom. There would be tapestries on the wall and a roaring fire in the middle for warmth and cooking.

Churls were poorer and lived in huts with thatched roofs. Animals lived inside with them and it would often be very cramped.

THE VIKINGS

Where did they live?

Viking longships brought families who settled in villages. There were farmers, who kept animals and grew crops. They tended to all live together in a building called a 'longhouse'. England was much more fertile than their homelands, which often flooded. The longhouses were built from wood or stone and had a thatched roof on top. Again, like the Anglo-Saxons they kept some animals inside.

Religion

Among the many gods the Vikings believed in, two of the most interesting were Thor, the God of Thunder and the mischievous Loki, who could shapeshift into different animals.

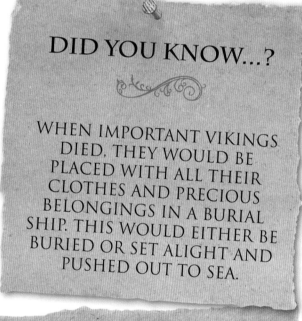

DID YOU KNOW...?

WHEN IMPORTANT VIKINGS DIED, THEY WOULD BE PLACED WITH ALL THEIR CLOTHES AND PRECIOUS BELONGINGS IN A BURIAL SHIP. THIS WOULD EITHER BE BURIED OR SET ALIGHT AND PUSHED OUT TO SEA.

THE NORSE GOD, LOKI.

What did the Anglo-Saxons and the Vikings LEAVE BEHIND?

The Anglo-Saxons left many influences in England. Parts of our language are from Anglo-Saxon words and names of places, such as London and Winchester. A place-name ending in 'ham', shows it was once a settlement. 'Ham' meant village.

West Stow & SUTTON HOO

There are many sites where Anglo-Saxon settlements have been discovered. West Stow is an Anglo-Saxon village that has been recreated and modelled on archaeological finds. This has allowed us to gain a fascinating insight in to who the Anglo-Saxons were and how they lived.

Sutton Hoo is another example of an archeological discovery. Archaeologists discovered a burial mound containing a ship filled with the possessions of an important leader. They knew he was an important leader as he had many expensive possessions buried with him. One of the items they discovered was a helmet that would have been worn by a warrior.

Structures

Some Anglo-Saxon churches remain, like this one in Dover. The church was built next to a Roman tower. This is a great example of different invaders adding on to already existing structures which previous conquerors of England have left behind.

THE VIKING Legacy

Similarly to the Anglo-Saxons, the Vikings left behind a legacy. Archaeologists often find remains of burial sites, carvings and even treasure.

DID YOU KNOW...?

VIKINGS USED MEASUREMENTS, SUCH AS THE DOZEN, THAT ARE STILL USED TO THIS DAY.

Language

Vikings also had a clear influence on the English language. Words such as egg, law and knife are all of Old Norse origin. Place names also tell us if Vikings lived there. Places ending in 'thorpe' or with an 'ay' are likely to have been settled in by the Vikings.

Can you think of any other place names that the Vikings may have lived in?

The Gokstad

The Gokstad, is a Viking ship discovered in A.D. 1880, in Norway. It was enclosed within a burial mound that had been built with turf. The ship was almost 24 metres long and 5 metres wide. A powerful Viking, who died in around A.D. 900, was buried within the ship. Archaeologists found that the man inside had injuries consistent with battle.

DID YOU KNOW...?

BURIED WITH THE VIKING MAN IN THE GOKSTAD WERE THE REMAINS OF TWELVE HORSES, EIGHT DOGS AND TWO PEACOCKS, AS WELL AS LOTS OF TREASURE!

REPLICA OF THE GOKSTAD

TIMELINE

Romans

A.D. 43 – The Romans successfully invaded Britain.

A.D. 401-410 – The Romans withdraw from Britain: Anglo-Saxon people begin to settle.

A.D. 779 – Mercia becomes the most powerful Anglo-Saxon kingdom.

A.D. 617 – Northumbria becomes the most powerful Anglo-Saxon kingdom.

A.D. 600 – Much of Britain is now under Anglo-Saxon control.

Vikings

Around A.D. 789 – The first recorded Viking attacks on Britain take place.

A.D. 793 – Vikings attack the monastery at Lindisfarne.

Around 850 A.D. – Viking raiders begin to settle.

Around A.D. 865-877 – Viking Army known as 'The Great Heathen' army invades Britain.

A.D. 866 – Vikings captured modern day York and named their capital Jorvik. The North of England is now part of Danelaw.

The Norman victory ends Anglo-Saxon rule in England.

14th October A.D. 1066 – The Battle of Hastings: William of Normandy defeats Harold and becomes King of England.

A.D. 410 – The Romans left Britain.

A.D. 410-450 – The 'Dark Ages'.

Anglo-Saxons

A.D. 450 – 750 Britain is divided up into the Kingdoms of Northumbria, Mercia, Wessex, Essex, Sussex and Kent.

A.D. 450 – Anglo-Saxons begin to invade Britain.

A.D. 871 – King Alfred defeats the Vikings, but allows them to settle in Eastern England, also under Danelaw.

A.D. 892 – Vikings' second invasion to fight King Alfred of Wessex.

A.D.1016 – King Canute of Denmark captures the English Crown.

A.D.1042 – Edward the Confessor becomes King.

Normans

28th September A.D. 1066 – Normans invade! Victorious Harold Godwinson travels with his army to Hastings.

25th September A.D. 1066 – The Battle of Stamford Bridge. Harold Godwinson defeats Harald Hardrada.

KINGS OF ENGLAND

ANGLO-SAXON

Offa, King of Mercia (A.D. 757-796) the most powerful Anglo-Saxon Kingdom at this point in time.

Egbert, King of Wessex (A.D. 802-839) became king when the Anglo-Saxon kingdom of Wessex became the most powerful kingdom.

Ethelwulf (A.D. 839-856) son of Egbert.

Ethelbald (A.D. 856-860) the oldest son of Ethelwulf.

Ethelbert (A.D. 860-866) Ethelbald's brother.

Ethelred (A.D. 866-871) another son of Ethelwulf.

Alfred 'The Great' (A.D. 871-899) fifth son of Ethelwulf.

Edward 'The Elder' (A.D. 899-924) Alfred the Great's son.

Ethelstan (A.D. 924-939) Edward's heir to the throne.

Edmund I (A.D. 939-946) Athelstan's half-brother, claimed the throne as he did not have a son.

Edred (A.D. 946-55).

Edwy (A.D. 955-959) Edmund's oldest son.

Edgar (A.D. 959-975) King of Mercia and Danelaw inherited the throne from his brother.

Edward II 'The Martyr' (A.D. 975-979) the sudden death of Edgar led to his oldest son Edward becoming King.

Ethelred II 'The Unready' (A.D. 979-1013 and 1014-1016) youngest son of Edgar was seven when he inherited the throne.

VIKING

Sweyn (A.D. 1013-1014) Viking invader (Danish) Sweyn took power from the young Ethelred, his reign was very short!

Edmund II 'Ironside' (A.D. Apr – Nov 1016) son of Ethelred, made himself ruler of Danelaw. Defeated by Canute. They struck a treaty, allowing Edmund to rule Wessex and Canute the rest.

Canute 'The Great' (A.D. 1016-1035) became undisputed King of England in 1016.

Harold Harefoot (A.D.1035-1040) son of Canute, ruled Mercia and Northumbria.

Hardicanute (A.D. 1040-1042) was the King of Wessex from 1035 until the death of his half-brother Harold in 1040, when he became the King of England.

Edward III 'The Confessor' (A.D. 1042-1066) surviving son of Ethelred.

Harold II (A.D. Jan – Oct 1066).

Edgar Atheling (A.D. Oct – Dec 1066) grandson of Edmund Ironside.

NORMAN

William I 'The Conqueror' (A.D. 1066-1087) the first Norman King of England, reigning from 1066 until his death in 1087.

GLOSSARY

Authority: Someone in charge.

Britons: The first people to live in Britain.

Barbarian: People who rebelled against the laws of the land.

Celts: Another term for Britons, native people to Britain.

Census: A record of people living in a land.

Conquered: To take control of a place.

Constantinople: Wealthiest city of the Roman Empire, became the capital of the Byzantine Empire.

Decline: A gradual and continuous loss of strength.

Emperor: A person that rules an empire.

Exiled: Officially sent away from home.

Extensive: Covering a large area.

Fortresses: A building or group of buildings to protect an area, eg. a city.

Heir: A person who inherits from someone, does not have to be a family member.

Hereditary: Passed on from family.

Invaders: A person or group that invades a country, region, or other place.

Looted: Steal goods during a war.

Native: A person born in a specific place.

Monasteries: A building or buildings occupied by a community of monks living under relgious vows.

Monks: A religious person.

Pagans: A person holding religious beliefs other than those of the main world religions.

Picts: Ancient people who lived in Scotland.

Raids: A surprise attack.

Reeve: A local person of power.

Resistance: Defending an area.

Seafaring: A person who travels by sea.

Tapestries: A piece of fabric with designs or pictures on. Usually woven and used as decoration

Treaty: An agreement between people.

Traditions: Something that is passed down from person to person over time.

Tribes: A group of people, or a community with similar values, interests or relations.

INDEX

Photo Credits

Photocredits: Abbreviations: l-left, r-right, b-bottom, t-top, c-centre, m-middle. All images are courtesy of Shutterstock.com, unless stated otherwise.

Front Cover – Khosro, 2 – jmv (https://www.flickr.com/photos/jmv/1281973148), 4b – Justin Black, 4r – jeff gynane, 5t – Peter Hermes Furian, 5t – Peter Hermes Furian, 5br – meunierd, 6tl – gmstockstudio, 7l – Bildagentur Zoonar GmbH, 7r – Danny Smythe, 7br – Asmus Koefoed, 8tr – Algol, 11tr – Peter Lorimer, 11l – GTS Productions, 11br – York Museum Trust (https://commons.wikimedia.org/wiki/File:Gilling_Sword_-_hilt_-_YORYM_1977_51.JPG), 12 – Khosro, 15tr – Andrew Barker, 15b – Philip Bird LRPS CPAGB, 16tr – Elena Mirage, 18bl – symbiot, 18tr – SeraphP, 20b – Kevin Eaves, 23b – jorisvo, 24b – Peter Lorimer, 25tr – ricochet64, 25b – Vuk Kostic, 26tl – Ziko-C (https://commons.wikimedia.org/wiki/File:2004_sutton_hoo_01.JPG), 26b – Magdanatka.